REME[...]

An Alzheimer's Journey
Through Art and Poetry

Cheryl Kempner

Artwork by

Sandy Feldmus

ISBN (paperback): 978-1-7379510-0-1

Editing, formatting & cover design by
Our Galaxy Publishing, LLC

For Marc, Jared, Ethan and Ari

For Mom and Dad

Much love, thank you xo

foreword

Remember Me is an anthology honoring my mother living with Alzheimer's. This collection tracks her disease through her artwork and my poetry. It follows the beauty of her creations and the subsequent decline of her artistry over the years.

The double entendre of REMEMBER is a way to express how those inflicted with the devastating amoeba that is Alzheimer's disease would hope that they can remember, but we remember for them. We remember the moments, the stories, the person they were, the person they are, and the person they have become. They have shaped and molded who we are by being part of our lives. We are the **ME**.

I hope I am remembered by my mom, and of course, by my husband and children. I want to make my mark on the world.

This work is also a culmination of my life experiences. A move from New York to New Jersey when I was 13 years old, losing my first grandparent at 16, family betrayal, family love, and my feelings and observations while following my mother's journey through the tangled world of dementia. Finally, the trauma I experienced in a major car accident left me with a visible scar.

But, despite it all, I say, "I am fine." I say, "I am okay." I say, "I am good." I seek to share my feelings and experiences and hope to connect with others that may hide their emotions. If I could help one person, touch one person's soul, connect with one person, then I have achieved my goal.

As the **ME**, our obligation as family, friends, and humans is to relate to these victims' encounters. This collection seeks to explore the feelings and thoughts of people living with Alzheimer's, the caregivers' truths, and the individual plight.

I can tell you firsthand, everyone's journey is unique, and every family is different. This collection is our family's story. Unlike most patients, my mom stopped talking. She communicates with her eyes and at times sticks out her tongue in jest. She's docile, sits in a chair, does not scream or curse anymore. The lack of interaction and communication makes spending time with her long and challenging. Since she can't speak, I can only imagine what she is thinking. Hence the chapter entitled "Through My Eyes" reflects pieces told through her eyes.

This disease has taken a mental and emotional toll on those caring for the individual as loved ones and caregivers. Imagine how the spouse feels after spending a lifetime with a person who does not remember their life together, or the children who have a living parent that is not "there." Think of the aide who spends 24 hours a day, seven days a week, nursing the patient, only to be integrated with a strange family and receive no validation from the one cared for. These are the people for who "Through Their Eyes" is written for.

And, finally, "What About Me?" is for the child in me who still has feelings about my unfinished relationship with my parent, and who needs to express herself in some forum. It is for the person suffering another hardship yet still needs to take this Alzheimer's journey with a family member.

This book is a lifelong dream. Without the love, devotion,

and patience of my family, this could not have been birthed.

To Marc, I may not say it enough or ever, but I truly appreciate all that you do for me, for us, for the world. To Jared, Ethan, and Ari, I love you with all of my heart. Your devotion to your grandma, your weekly visits, interactions, singing, helping her navigate her world, including her in events, and joking with her has not gone unnoticed. To Ari, my weekly companion and compadre, I have witnessed your unbridled passion for your grandma. Sitting on her lap, making her laugh when she can't, flashing her so she smiles, speaking to her eyes, feeding her—you are my dedicated strength. My family, you are a blessing to all that have the privilege of connecting with the squad. Xo

To my friends who have had a weekly glimpse into my words, thank you, you know who you are. To my parents, Sandy and Sam, much love, strength and gratitude. To my mom, Sandy, your journey has not gone unnoticed. Your strength is real. I know you are in there. I believe you want to find ME. I hope this book makes you proud and understood.

To all of you struggling with a loved one with memory loss, dementia, Alzheimer's, stay the course. They are in there. I am here. xoxo

Cheryl Kempner

Dementia and Artwork

These pictures are a representation of the decline in artwork of a person with dementia. My mom's talent and creativity evolved into the beautiful, colorful still life art portrayed in this book.

The small town she painted in 1974, which is the most symbolic representation of comfort and family, is so elaborate with attention to detail. She painted the fishing wharf over 15 years ago.

We see the decline in ability in the subsequent pictures of a house, so simple and childlike, then the capacity to draw halted, and coloring in the lines was a chore. Seven years into this disease, my mom cannot even hold a pencil, the tool that defined her business sense, creativity, and logical mind. So, for those who cannot envision what this disease can do, these pictures show the functional decline of a person with dementia.

REMEMBER

THROUGH MY EYES

Red, yellow, green, blue.
Red, yellow, green, blue.

The pallet of a life that used to be.
The colors painted on the canvas,
And then it struck.
The colors started bleeding into each other.
Red into orange and orange into yellow.
The vivid sharp shapes became abstract
scribbles of a still life.
Searching for color but it's now a black pen.
Color in the lines.

In the lines, in letters, words, boxes,
No abstract, no design, just scribble.
With each stroke something is lost.
Each line a mission to complete a thought.
A passion to leave a mark.
Color. There is no color.

Everything is black and white.
Red, yellow, green, blue is gone.

Passion

Sandy
'24

Please be my memory, my guide, my eyes.
Please be my memory and remember, I'm wise.
I was bright and funny before I got sick.
I'm the person I was, but I cannot think as quick.

Remember for me your childhood and youth.
Remember for me when you lost your first tooth.
Remember for me your graduation day.
Remember for me all the things I would say.

Remember for me I am your mother.
Remember for me you have no other.
For I am still here, although I don't know.
I am still here, you reap what you sow.

Your wedding, your children, holidays and more.
Remember for me what was in my core.
The songs, the stories, the prayers, my life.
Remember for me I was a wife.
A wife, a mother, a sister, a friend.
A daughter, an artist, this isn't the end.
Remember for me I had a home.
Remember for me what I used to own.

My house, my cars, my trips of yore.
Remember for me the things I adore.
My art, my cards, my games and travel.
Remember for me before I unravel.
Somewhere down deep, I know it's still there.
Remember for me so I know you still care.

Some Days

Some days, she's present and in the know
Some days, she laughs and goes with the flow
Some days, she appears to know who I am
Some days, I don't know if I give a damn
Some days, she feeds herself, some days she's fed
Some days, she tired and can't hold up her head
Some days, I visit, and she tries to walk
Some days, I visit, and we sit and talk
Some days, she smiles, and her eyes are clear
Some days, her face is covered in fear
Some days, I feel she can see my soul
Some days, I wonder what is the goal
Some days, she looks at pictures and blinks
Some days, she flirts with her grandsons and winks
Some days, I think she eats too much
Some days, I wonder if it's only a crutch
Some days, her mouth is open and out of place
Some days, she sits and stares into space
Some days, we listen to music and hope she can stand
Some days, there's nothing and I hold her hand
Some days, she holds her baby doll so near
Some days, I wish she would call me dear
Some days, she fakes it really well
Some days, it feels like we're going through hell
Some days, I wonder if she is scared
Some days, I wonder if she will be spared
Some days, he looks at her with such love
Some days, I wonder what's up above

Pistachios and Pencils

Pistachios and pencils
What an odd combination
Pistachios and pencils
Defining life's conflicting station
We found them in the pantry, hidden away
Like the secrets of her life, she's always kept at bay

How telling it is that these are the things
Hidden away with all that life brings
Her two favorite pastimes were coloring and eating
Her two favorite pastimes are now just fleeting

The pencils and pens she cannot hold
The colors run from pastel to bold
Outside the lines, she scribbles and tries
Outside the lines, as her life just flies

The artist she was is long forgotten
The days of expression have just turned rotten
But the works remain shining so bright
The works remain, they depict the light
The light of a life that was full of color
The light of a life that's like no other

The pistachio nuts, now that's the pleasure
Of my mother's love for her daily treasure
Snacks and chocolate were her go-to
Now she needs help and can barely chew

Life comes full circle to expose what was hidden
Life comes full circle to what is forbidden
Pistachios and pencils
Are all that remain
Pistachios and pencils clutter the brain

Dementia

Tangles, plaques, neurons
The brain's shriveling tissue
Lost in a black hole.

Shrinking, shrinking, shrinking
Forever shrinking brain
Until one day it is no more
No more thoughts, words, actions, feelings, doings

No more

No more walking
No more smiling
Just sleeping
Eyes so heavy
It takes every ounce of energy to open them

Are you there?
Open your eyes
Wake up
It's me
Wake up
Where has she gone?
Is she in there?
Can she hear me?
Is she trapped?
Or just asleep?

Her heart beats
Her organs work
The amoeba eats away at her brain
It's not time
More things need to be said
It's too sudden
Sudden changes are not good
She will come back
Open your eyes

23

A Visit

It's just the beginning
Three years in
She knows my name

She opens the door but does not lock it behind her
She tries to find a place for the new picture I gave her
She said she'd move things later
I said, let's do it now
It's perfect she says

She asks if we want a drink
We say later
We try to chat
There's little conversation
She asks if we want a drink
We say yes
She tries to find the glasses
She opens the cabinets
She finds the right one
She gives me a glass
She gets me water
Her gait is off
She walks slowly
She's young, only 75

We sit at the table
What's new, I ask

Nothing she says
Where's your coloring?
I don't know

I cleaned up
The family room is spotless
I like things organized, she says
Are you playing cards?
Painting
Playing canasta tomorrow
Good, I say

Do you want to see the pictures from our cruise, I ask?
Yes, she says
Let's slide through the pictures on my phone
Are you bored yet?
No, they are wonderful
Did you have a good time?
Great, I said

How are you feeling
She says, I'm good
You lost a lot of weight, I said
Yes, she says
What do you eat?
Eggs with...with...
I said tomatoes, cheese, spinach
Give me a minute
I say, lox
I found it hidden on the side of the refrigerator
She says, yes, Nova

She offers more snacks.
She takes chocolate.
Are you allowed to have that?
She says she can do what she wants
We sit again
We look at more pictures
Do you remember when we went to Venice
She smiles
Did you buy anything, she asks?

Not much, I said
Some souvenirs, I had an amazing time, though
She holds her head in her hands and looks at my pictures
I know it's enough

She tells me they just came back from a trip
There was no trip
She tells me dad left at 3 o'clock for cards
I spoke with him at 5:30
They were having dinner
I know it's enough

She wants to change and watch TV
I say maybe we will do this again next Thursday
She says sure if she has no plans
I said okay, lock the door
We kiss goodbye
Thanks for coming
Lock the door
Click

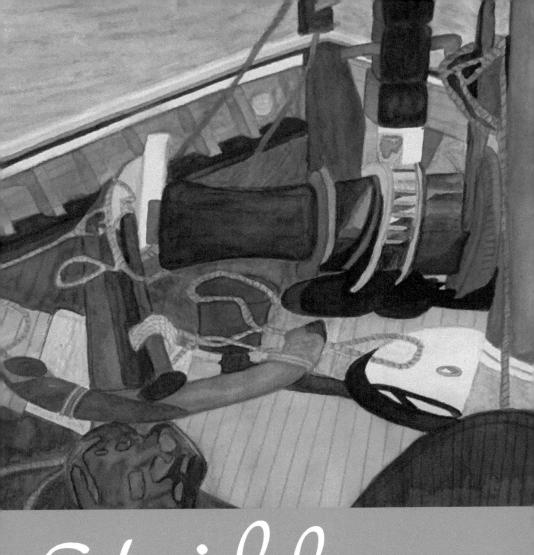

still

life

Sitting standing walking no talking
Sitting standing walking no talking
Sitting standing walking no talking

Where has she gone?
Where is she now?
She's here, but not
Like a body without a soul
Or a soul without a mind
Sitting gazing
Gazing at what?
What does she think?
What does she see?
Is she in there?
Where is she?
What happened to my mother?

Sitting standing walking no talking
How much longer will she know my name?
How much longer will she know of my existence?
How much longer will she know me?

How much longer will she be
Sitting standing walking no talking?

The days are long and quiet
The questions are repetitive
The answers are the same
The stare is empty
She is dazed
The smile is gone
What are you thinking?
Are you in there?
Sitting standing walking no talking

No laughter
No conversation
No focus
No comprehension
No memories
No nothing

Sitting standing walking no talking

An August Night

We went for a visit.
She looked and stared.
She did not know
It was me, I feared.

We tried to talk,
Do puzzles, and dance.
Music or color, there was no chance.

Let's try Sinatra, Fiddler, Streisand and more,
Will anything trigger the memories before.

She sat so stoic,
And did not blink.
She sat so stoic,
And did not think.

Gazing into space,
Nothing is there.
Gazing into space,
It's just not fair.

Her eyes are glossy.
Her arms are folded.
Sitting and staring at the TV,
And then she scolded.

She scolded at me, as if I was five.
She scolded at me, as she came alive.
Something was triggered, I don't know what.
Something was triggered, it's in her gut.

Within a moment, the woman changed,
From my mother to the one estranged.

Leave my house,
Leave me alone.
Leave my house,
No one is home.

I don't want you here,
You must leave.
I don't want you here,
You must believe.

No reasoning or hugs would calm her down,
Or have her believe she wasn't to drown.

We came to visit and provide some love,
But her thoughts and actions come from above.
She has no control over what she does,
I'm sure she's sorry and regrets what was.

But she's not the mom I once knew,
She's the mom that's since withdrew.
The scolding and staring is not really her,
What she is now, is just a blur.

It's a baby boy, she says with a smile
It's the only full sentence we've heard in a while
I forgot her voice, tone, and sound
Despite our tries, she is not around

But now, with love and attention, she laughs and smiles
Her eye light up, which we haven't seen in a while
So, we gave her a doll, dressed in blue
She hugged it and held it like she always knew

She cuddled and cradled its head in her hand
Almost as though she found a pebble in sand
What did we tap into?
What do you know?
The natural instinct can never go

While she cannot feed herself, walk, or talk
A little baby doll can make her squawk
With delight and joy and hope for tomorrow
That this baby doll is the time we wanted to borrow

That was yesterday and today's a new day
But the baby doll she's holding the very same way
So, the primitive instinct is there for the caring
The love of a baby doll is the key to us bearing
This terrible disease of the mind and the brain
But the heart and soul always remain.

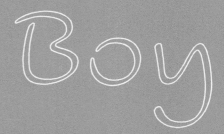

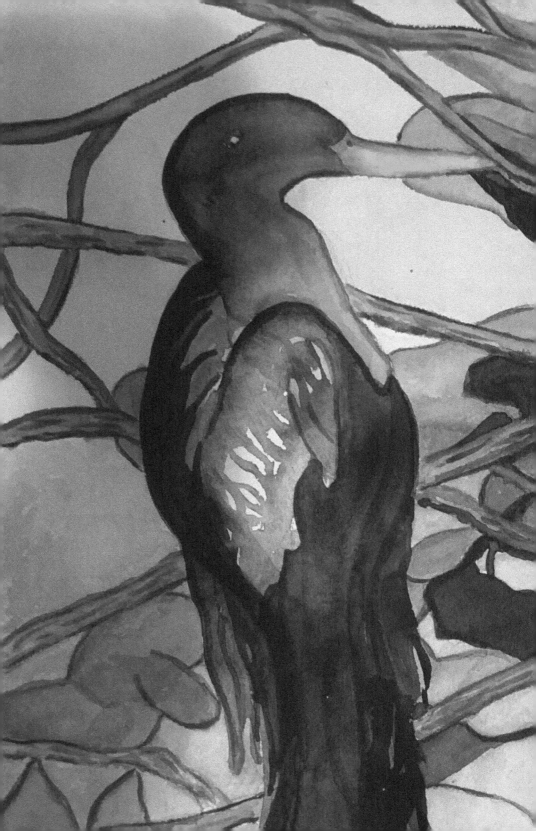

All Day in a Chair

All day in a chair
She watches TV
All day in a chair
What does she see?

Staring at the walls, examining her hands
Is this a way to live? These were not her plans
No one calls, as time goes by
Maybe they're afraid, or don't want to pry

How lonely an existence must this be
If it was me, I'd want to flee
But we come to visit a few times a week
We come to visit and we try to speak

Repeat, repeat repeat your name
Repeat, repeat, this is not a game

Not a sound or a grimace, there's nothing to say
Every single day goes the same way

Until we sing Happy Birthday to you,
She comes alive like she used to do.
She remembers the words
We hear her voice
She remembers the words
And we all rejoice

It becomes the ritual, the go-to song
A way to connect, a way to belong
In her world, in another land
In her world where she leads the band

Then we gave her a doll to try to connect
We gave her a doll and little did we expect
That she would love this doll like she was a mother
That she would love this doll like there was no other

She kisses the doll and holds it so tight
She kisses the doll and her eyes turn bright
The baby, the baby, that she once knew
The baby, the baby, then she says boo

Sitting on her lap and making jokes
Tossing balloons as we try to coax
The mother, the grandmother, the wife that existed
Just make an appearance, my heart insisted

We keep on trying to enter her space
We know we've arrived when we see her face
A smile, a spark tells us that
We have connected with a place, a place she's at.

Sandy Feldmus 2012

Her Celebration

Sitting on the outside looking in
I see my birthday celebration about to begin
I know he's been planning this for weeks
I know normalcy is what he seeks

The guests arrive and I sit and stare
I'm all dressed up and they've done my hair
Like their little doll they seek to mold
Wishing so much that I would unfold

Food, drink, balloons and presents galore
Gifts to unwrap, there is more in store
The conversations abound in the room
Like I'm here but I'm not, I'm in the womb

The party goes on like I am alive
But I can't take part, I cannot arrive
They try so hard to get me out
Talking and singing, pictures about

But do they know I understand?
Trapped in my body, this was not planned
I try to get the words out
The thoughts, the smiles have no route
Blink your eyes, let them know
That I am here and love them so

Gifts are given to me by hand
My fingers won't move, my soul is bland
There is no strength in my head
Close your eyes, you're almost dead

I try to come around
Today is my day to be crowned
The birthday queen, that's what they want
For me to be their debutant

But not right now, I cannot play
I cannot muster up the strength today
Let me sleep, let me rest
Today's a day, not a test

Who would have guessed ten years ago?
This is the way the wind would blow
They bring me some cake on a dish
I close my eyes and make a wish

Oh, if I could only let them know
I acknowledge this is a show
For them to feel good about themselves
Just check your egos on the shelves

I'm the one looking out from within
I'm the one that cannot win

The day has ended and they still strive
For me to try to come alive
On a pillow, I lay my head
Enough already, it's time for bed

Nothing

To sit and stare at the walls
A feeling of emptiness in your life
Something is missing
Is it people or things?
You cannot quite put your finger on it
But you know it's there
Enough to make you crazy

Running up the driveway in time to see
Grandma is standing and waiting for me.
With a big bright smile and hugs galore,
With treats of candy and love in store.

I love my grandma.
We can talk and talk.
We look at the flowers as we take a walk.
We play cards, tag, and bake cookies together.
Stories and fun times that last forever.
Tickles and laughter, singing and more,
Until it's time for me to leave and close the door.

But grandma, one day, I came, and your eyes were sad,
At first, I thought you were really mad.
But then, I realized nothing was there.
Your eyes were empty, and all you did was stare.

We try to color in my old coloring books,
Holding pencils and markers, you give me strange looks.
Do you know who I am or am I a stranger to you?
We try to do puzzles, but you can only do a few.

Let's sing a song or try to dance.
Please give my grandma another chance.

It's hard for me to visit and see her this way,
But she is my grandma, so I will stay.
I can hold her hand and sit for a while.
Talk about school and make her smile.
My grandma is always in my heart.
This horrible disease cannot tear us apart.

She Has a Boyfriend

I hear she has a boyfriend, he has no name
I hear she has a boyfriend, it's not a game
I hear she has a boyfriend, she won't tell us where
I hear she has a boyfriend, she waits for him out there

She wanders outside
He has to know
That her boyfriend's inside and she must go

What must he think?
How must he feel?
She has a boyfriend, and he's not real
But she is his, and he is hers
Beyond this life, maybe she does

What is she thinking?
Is there anything there?
What is she thinking?
Dare we compare?
It's her life now and we do not know
What the mind triggers or how it may grow

Is there more to what we think?
Is there life beyond her blink?
A world trapped in her mind
Memories that only she can find

She cannot share her heart's delight
She barely smiles day or night

The mind is fierce
The mind is strong
It creates a world where the days are long
Imagination is the game
Memories are no longer to blame
She has a boyfriend who has no name
She has a boyfriend it's not a game

I Am

Do you see me?
I am here
Do you see me?
I can hear
I can hear every word you say
Just because I can't answer in a certain way

Do you see me?
I am here
Do you see me?
I can hear

You ask how I am
I look and stare
I try to get the words out, but they're just not there

How do you feel, what's going on?
You smile and wonder, where have I gone?

I can still feel
I'm happy and sad
I can still feel
When you visit I'm glad

I'm glad you came to see me today
I'm glad you recall I did things a certain way

Let's look at pictures, do a puzzle or watch TV
Whatever we do, just sit next to me
I feel you near me
I know you are there
I just can't tell you how much I care

In my body and in my soul
Can you see me?
I don't know

I'm in front of you, you have to know
I'm not invisible
Don't let me go

I am still alive
I have a pulse
I have a heart
It beats so strong
I have a brain
It just does not work as long

Can you see me? I am here.
Can you see me? I can hear.

Hold Me

Hold me tight because you'll never know
The fear inside as I rock to and fro
I'm so alone, locked away in there
I'm so alone. Do you know I'm here?

I can see your face, but it's a stranger I see
I feel your presence next to me
I'm afraid to sit, afraid to stand
Just sit with me and hold my hand

I hold some beads, some cloth and yarn
I watch TV, listen to music, and don't give a darn
I'm staring at the walls, the paintings I've made
Life is a blur, I'm in an arcade

So many distractions, so much going on
I sit and stare, my memory is gone
They ask if I know them, I do not know
They look for a sign, I have nothing to show

Stay with me for as long as you can
You'll be surprised, you'll have a plan
A way for me to come alive
Stay with me and I will thrive

My mind is gone, but I am not fake
Let me go and my heart will break
I am real, I need you here
Stay with me and hold me dear

Me

I know you are mine, please don't go far
You think I forgot who you are
I just can't find the words to say
I can no longer find my way

While my memories are gone and not complete
This does not mean it won. I won't concede to defeat
I don't care what I have been told
My mind is mine and I'm not too old

I still recall the day we met
The day you were born, I cannot forget

I know it's in me, some place down deep
I know it's in me, I'm sorry don't weep
But I feel the thoughts, the pain, and more
My eyes tear up, I can't recall the lore

Of our family, our history, it's all gone
I know you will live and move on

The names, the stories, the music and more
Is a blank in my mind and a closed door
Knock it down, I try and try
Knock it down, this is a lie

How did this happen?
A life is a blur
How does this happen?
How does this occur?

Was it the exercise, the sugar, or the genes?
Was it the luck of the draw or just the means?

Why chose me and not chose you?
Why chose me? Give me a redo

Is it just fate that this was the plan?
Is it just fate that no one gives a damn?

Do you really care that I am here?
That I just sit and I'm not clear

A mind a waste, a life a bore
A mind a waste, a life no more

the Message

Now the time has come, and I must be off
There are no more good mornings or good nights
The days are shorter, and the nights are longer
An everlasting sleep comes over me
While the irreversible force takes me
I'm too weak to fight it
So please don't cry when you all find out
That I'll no longer be there to kiss you goodnight
Or to answer your questions
Just remember how much I love you all
And that I'll guide you forever
May you all be grateful for the time you have left

[For Bubby Dora]

THROUGH THEIR EYES

You never know when it will be the last walk.
You never know when it will be the last talk.

Oh, she's still here, but she is not.
The life she knew, she's now forgot.

The days are long and blur into each other.
What in the world has happened to my mother?

She sits and stares at the TV with no regard.
The world still circles. It is so hard.

To see her hold on to a pen,
Like a lioness guarding her little cub's den.

As she folds her napkin like a shrine,
"Don't touch that, it is mine."

Collected memories kept in her pocket.
A lifetime of treasures inside a locket.

Her mind that remembers nothing we know.
A world of emotions that does not show.

Let's eat some fruit. Can she swallow?
Would she want us to sit and wallow?

In the world that has become a big empty house,
No noise, no talking, quiet as a mouse.

Then she drifts and falls asleep,
Breathing so heavy, breathing so deep,

Only to awake, "Are you okay?"
"Yes, of course," is all she can say.

As she repositions and sits and stares,
So robotic as she glares.

It's time to go, she says goodbye.
She doesn't get up, she doesn't try.

You never know when it will be the last walk.
You never know when it will be the last talk.

you Never Know

Don't Complain

Don't complain about the phone calls
Because you don't know when they will end
Don't complain about the crying
Because she'll never mend

Don't worry about the sheets because one day they'll be dry
Don't worry about not making sense because one day she'll only sigh
Don't think about the laundry, it will always be there
Don't think about the cooking, one day she'll only stare

Don't ask her if she remembers, you know she can't anymore
Don't ask if she knows you, the answer was given before
Just look into her eyes, and hold her hand
A glimmer of hope, if she smiles and tries to stand

Just sit and talk about today and not tomorrow
The time you have right now is here, and surely not to borrow
Make her laugh and make her smile, is all that we can do
Treat her like a newborn baby, whose every day's anew

But remember her experiences, her life that remains
The soul trapped inside of her, not the person we maintain
Everyone has a purpose, a reason to be here
Maybe hers was just a sacrifice, to keep us all so near

So, treasure the days she's here like there are no other
Because good or bad you only have one mother

The House

The house is empty, no one is home
The windows are dark, there is no place to roam
If the walls could talk, what would they say?
The laughs, the love, the joys of yesterday?

Seasons come and seasons go
The laughter, the tears with history in tow
The memories are there, they are not misplaced
The feelings and emotions are encased
Within your heart and who you are
No matter what, we won't go far

Do you remember holding me?
Do you remember when I was three?
What about kindergarten or first grade?
When being with you, my day was made

You pushed me aside, but it did not matter
The walls heard it all, my cries, my chatter

What would the plaster think and what would it say?
What seeps from the cracks, fear and dismay?
The house, it listened, it saw it all
The births, the parties when we all stood tall

The trying times, the fights and the yelling
The lives that were touched in this dwelling
The door is closed, you can't get through
The roof, the shelter, that was you

On Caregivers

Taking care of her is no easy task.
The silence is deafening, she has nothing to ask.
The longest of days, up at nine,
Cleaning and cooking, time is not mine.
Laundry and changing her are what I do.
A labor of love from me to you.

My compassion runneth over, I do care.
If it was me, I'd want someone to be there.
So, I take your yelling, your cursing at me.
I know from experience, it's all you can see.
I'm new to your family, your home and your life.
I'm trying to make everyone happy so there is no strife.

I know what comes next, but they don't know.
I'm really your companion, not your foe.
I'll take this journey with you, my friend.
I'm with you as we round the bend.
In my heart, and in my soul,
Taking care of you is my goal.

[For Patricia]

She's ♥ Mine

I wonder how it feels to live with someone for 50 years,
The good, the bad, and all the tears.
Are the memories there, or did they fade away?
Does she realize I'm here with her every day?

We had our dreams, but never did I think
This would happen or she wouldn't blink.
That time would stand still every day,
That we wouldn't enjoy the rest of the way.

The way we planned to travel and to adore,
To reap the rewards of our hard work and more,
But I am for her and she is for me.
Whatever happens, will be what will be.

Sometimes I wonder if she remembers me.
Does she recall our journeys or the future we'd see?
Our laughter, our love, our missions galore.
Is this my life now? Every day is a chore?

I promised to keep her happy and safe.
She knew this was coming. Try to keep the faith.
We had a plan. I'd take care of her,
I agreed to do this, but the days are a blur.

I owe her so much. She was there for me.
She followed my dreams to succeed and be free.
To work and create and spend all of our days
Building a business, but that's all a haze.

She doesn't remember all that we did.
How we struggled and sacrificed, the secrets we hid.
Does it matter now? I do not know.
All I know is it was just a show.

Sometimes I wonder what would be
If I ran away and it would just be me.
Does anyone think this would be wrong?
Would anyone know and sing my song?

Does she remember my name, my face, or my smile?
Or am I just another person who's there for a while?
Would she even care if I was not here?
For a day, a week, a month, or a year?
She doesn't know anymore,
If I was to stay or walk out the door.

The pain is real. It's not what I planned.
But this is the life. We have been banned.

I'll do what it takes to get us through
Because you are for me and I am for you.

[For Dad]

69

He
Wonders

Sometimes I wonder what she's thinking
Why this is happening? Why her brain is shrinking?
Why all the memories are fading away
Like nothing existed, not one single day

I wonder if she remembers all of our words
The cry of a child, the song of the birds
The words I've spoken, the good and the bad
Most of all, the love that we had

Does she remember our travels, and our walks?
Our children, our business, our love, and our talks?
You held me up and were my support
The dreams that we had all fell so short

To this stranger that invaded our life
Go begone, you cut like a knife
You robbed us of the last of years
You won the battle, a family in tears

Sometimes I wonder, does it all really matter?
Or is life a joke with memories to scatter

[For Dad]

Marry Me

"Will you marry me?", I propose
To my mother, that's all she knows
To laugh and smile, it could be worse
She could cry and yell and even curse
But she just smiles and holds her head
When we wake her up, she sits on her bed

She sits and stares until we clean up what's messed
Like a child waiting to get dressed
She sits, bare-naked, showing her breasts
We play along and pass the tests
She laughs and laughs the time is priceless
Showing our boobies diverts the crisis

Into the shower, we get her to go
The trepidation and fear are apparent, you know
She thinks she's walking into a bottomless pit
The unknown is before her until she can sit
She's reborn in the water, fresh and clean
Get up and get out, she sits like a queen

Perfectly dressed, her hair all curled
As though she was going out into the world
But her world is here at the kitchen table
A breakfast of fruit and eggs is all that she's able
To be fed by another's very kind hand
Her life is sinking in a dome of quicksand

From the table, she returns to her chair
She sits holding beads and can only stare
An occasional laugh, while she watches TV
She loves the oldies, that's all she can see.

Does she know the visitors that come and sit?
Or does she not care? I must admit
But she sits and smiles and holds her beads
As he looks at her, his heart bleeds

What happened to the woman he used to know?
His partner and the one who shares the show
She cannot stand, cook, or clean
Her life is his, it's just too mean
To end it all just like this
A half a century of love and wedded bliss

The cards just dealt a different hand
He was meant to be her support. This is not what he planned
Life goes on in such a way
It's a lot to watch all in a day
Life goes on in such a way
It's a lot to live through years of dismay

Last Night

Ready for bed, she sits and stares
We're in another room, no one cares
Called in to wish her a good night
But what we witnessed was quite a sight

We gave up on the fact that she would walk
That she would stand, color, or talk
But she picked herself up off of the bed
As though for a moment, she was in her head

I held her hand as she tried to walk
One foot, then the other, watching me like a hawk
Not knowing why or where we were going
We walked in a circle, her smile was glowing

Was this the time to test her mind?
Do I ask if she knows me or is this unkind?
But she's having a moment and maybe she knows
That I am the one, the one that she shows

So, I ask her my name, I look into her eyes
I ask her my name. Repeat me, she tries
She looks and listens and tries so hard
To repeat my name, the words are marred

She sounds it out in disbelief
Her voice was robbed by a vicious thief
But in her eyes, I can tell she knows it's me
She mouths my name, but only I can see

Around we turn to sit on her bed
I look into her eyes, I hold her head
I know you're in there, please come out
I know you're in there, I want to shout

What's my name? I ask once again
Thinking the moment will stay, but then
She says in a soft little voice
Sandra, that's her name. We all rejoice

She holds my hand, she holds it tight
She knows it's me, I'm still in sight
What just happened? We don't know
But we had a moment, a memory to show.

Like a newborn that does not know
Or a toddler that does not grow
Her birthday came
Her birthday went
But she does not know what wishes were sent

The mind is fierce and out of sight
It does not know or care about the heart's plight
That we may need to keep moving on
Or maybe it knows that we must stay calm
For we would go mad if we really did know
That our mind was shrinking, and we could not
grow

To new levels of our early existence
Or is it aware of our soul's forever persistence?
Do the flowers, the wishes, the visits, or chocolate
cake
Mean anything inside or is it just fake?
The talks, the laughs, the pictures and more
Does it tell a story or is it knocking on a closed
door?
To make up for lost time in the last few years
Few years that to some, means many more tears

But to others, it's time to make memories to last
Moments to take, moments to grasp

The veil has been lifted
The wall is no more
The relationship is freed
The tension, old lore
Could there be a message in disguise?
Or is it just the unraveling of all the lies?

The mind is a vicious thing
It can take away a human being
We know what's what, but how do we deal
Not knowing what she can actually feel
Her birthday came, her birthday went
She does not know that wishes were sent

Her Birthday

Rosh Hashanah

2020

Another holiday come and gone
She sits at the table, yet we carry on
With the way things were supposed to be
As if she was present to celebrate with me

There's trepidation as we lift the wheelchair up the stairs
Like a regal queen with no cares
As the matriarch, she sits at the head of the table
Only there are no words of wisdom, as she is not able

Occupied by a leaf on a toy apple
She fidgets and pulls at it as we all grapple
With the idea that it's a holiday and she doesn't know
The wine, the challah, the candles that glow

It's time to celebrate fresh starts
Hoping she knows that she's in our hearts
This may be the last where she fits
At the head of the table, where she sits

Who shall live and who shall die?
What do we know? We don't know why
We laugh and smile, we talk about our year
We reminisce, as she sheds a tear

Inside, her body wants to go
Her mind can't make it, we all know
Taking pictures and videos for moments to last
Knowing that next year she'll be out of our grasp.

She forgot My Birthday

She forgot my birthday, and it's not okay.
I thought she'd remember me on this day.
She doesn't think of me anymore.
If I'm not present, does she know I'm the one she bore?

She forgot my birthday. I'm 54.
Will she remember me forever more?
Am I in her soul or in her heart?
For in her mind, I am not.

She forgot my birthday. I'm 54.
A wish, a card, a gift no more.
Does she even know how far I soar?
Is it about me or is it about her?
Either way, our lives are a blur.
Can she feel I'm hers, or she was mine?
I think not and it's not fine.
Time marches on and she will not know
The woman I've become, the life I sow.

It's as if she is not here, but she remains.
It's as if I'm not here, but I cannot feign
That she forgot my birthday,
And it's not okay.

That two worlds cannot collide,
Does she feel my love on the inside?

She forgot my birthday,
I'm 54.
Wishes for me are no more.

What Did You Say?

Wait, what did you say? Oh yes, I remember now
Where are we going again? Oh, I see now
What's your name? Oh yea, you're my granddaughter

Five years ago, she walked this world knowing it all
She talked in conversations, confident and standing tall
Smiled bright and always with a colored pencil in her hand
She would even come to play with me in the sand
We could play cards for hours
From dark nights to afternoon spring showers

She follows him because they are so connected
She wanders around until she is directed
Yes, he is my grandpa, her best friend, since day one
He takes care of her and his day is never done

What I try to do is to be there for my mom
She is always there to keep me calm
On the outside, she handles this as cool as ice
But on the inside, I think she feels like she's paying the price
She cries in secret, and I know she feels sad
Why wouldn't she? She has to watch her mom deteriorate and become
mad

She never grew up the way I did
She wasn't as close with her family when she was a kid
Walking through this world day by day
Now, she has nothing to say

Wait, what did you say? I can't remember
Where are we going again? I can't remember
What's your name? I can't remember

She will soon be gone, but not quite yet
But little does she know she is mentally gone and making me fret

So here is to the days that you are still alive
But when you leave us, I know your soul and arts will continue to thrive.

[Ari Kempner, Age 15]

Mother's Day
2020

Happy Mother's Day to my mom
I wish you a life of peace and no harm
To come to you at this time
When troubles seem to want to shine

But we are here for you to know
Despite it all, you will grow
Into the person you are meant to be
Your soul of beauty for all to see

That you are a mother, a grandmother too
Life is more than what this disease can do
It can take your mind but not your soul
Not your heart or end goal

Which is to be with your loved ones now
Life comes full circle, but we do not bow
Out of the dreams that you have made
Although you think they will fade

But we all know the dreams that are
We are here for you, near and far
To hold you up when you can't stand
To make sure that you will always land

In the arms of someone you love
A sign of peace from up above

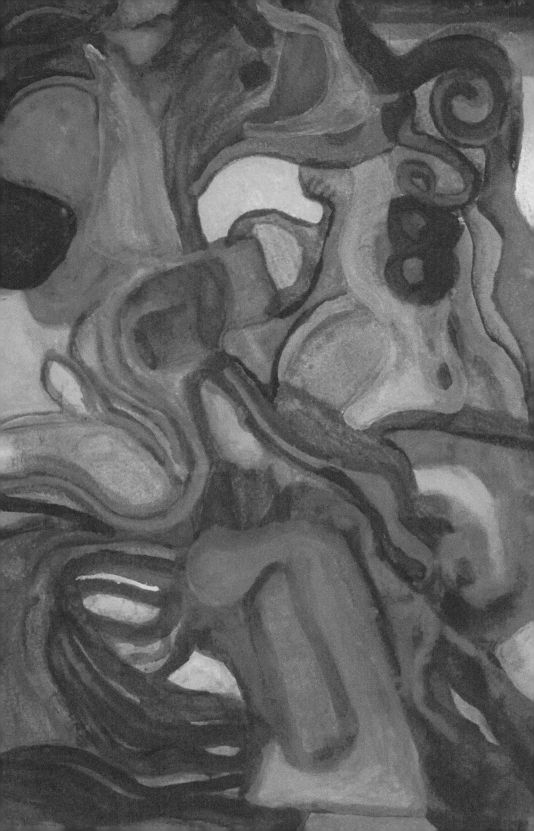

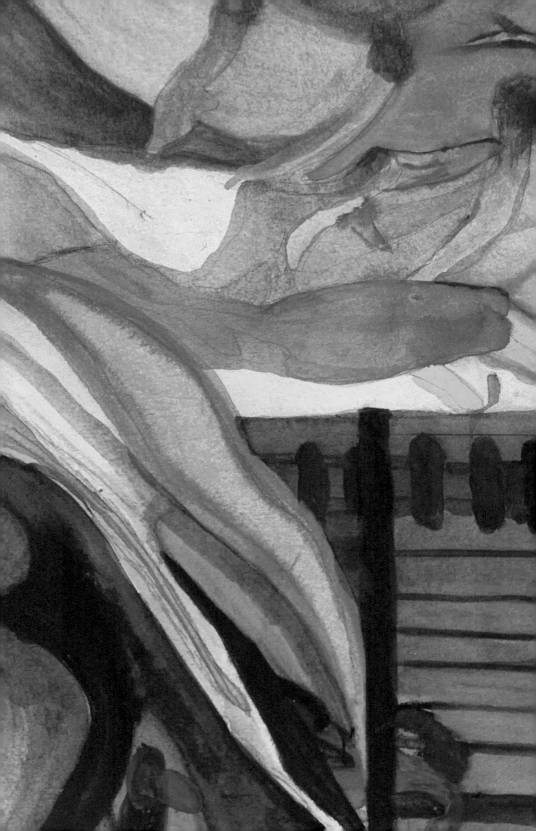

New Year's Eve

It's the last grasp for time
Only a few more minutes-
Seconds
So much has happened.
A life began,
A life has ended.
New joys,
New worries.
Some overjoyed with the future,
Others depressed with the past.
The clock has struck,
A year is gone,
A tear for the memories.
The sound of a horn,
Once again.

I Called Today

I called today
And she did not say
A word, a sound, or even a grunt
She smiled and waved, and the cues were so blunt

She's in there some place, so far away
She's hidden inside, and there she will stay
Safe from a world and powers that be
Away from us all and that's all that I see

For when I need a mom, she's not there
A smile, a glean, please just come here
To be the mom I need you to be
To be the one that asks about me

I know you're in there, please come out
A glimmer of hope, without a doubt

She's not there, nothing to be found
She's not there, but we are all around
For love and support
We won't go away
We are with you, to hold you, every day

I see it happening again
Another victim of the battle
I watch him walk
And
Listen to him talk

Slow and steady
I know its coming, the floodgates open
Sitting, standing, walking and talking

He talks, again
He calls her name; she comes
But he doesn't recall what he needs
He calls her name, again
She gets annoyed

The pattern repeats,
We know it's coming
How do you prepare?
Denial
How many years?
Two, Three, Four, Five

Learn from it or not
Driving, oh no, not the driving
Lost, forgetful, where are we going
Not in the dark

I can't
What's the plan
What do we do?
All alone on an island of despair

We're not alone, hundred's, thousand's of people
The same plight
Cries out for help
It's okay

He's sitting, standing, walking and talking
Time will tell
Maybe it will be different
Maybe it will be the same
We cannot do this again
Sitting, standing, walking and talking

Repeat

Repeat

Don't tell me how to think
Don't tell me how to feel
Don't tell me what is right
Don't tell me what is real

Until you walk in my shoes
And feel my heart break
Don't tell me what should be
As my soul's the one to ache.

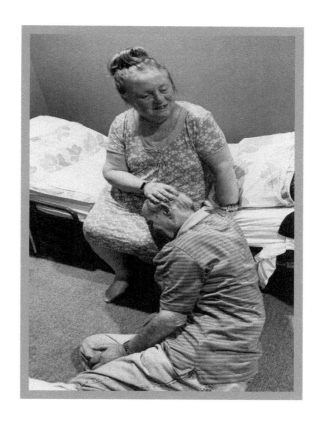

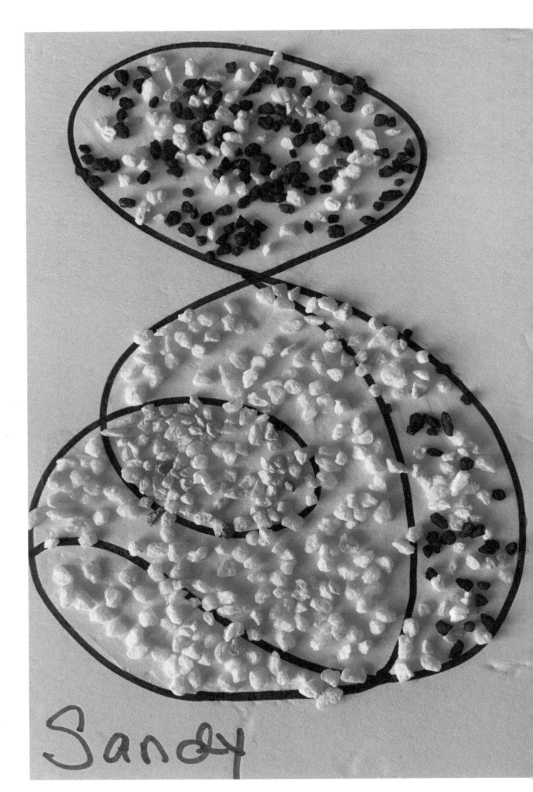

Sandy

WHAT ABOUT ME?

 Time

So bare she stands, so gray and old
Her arms come out and fingers fold

In the whispering whistles of the wind, she sways
Her soul is asleep through the dark, dreary days

No sign of life until behold
Her fingers once again unfold

Alas, becomes a new young sprout
Whose youthfulness is of no doubt

The shape of many youthful shades
Forms her fingers into long slender blades

She remains for as long as time will allow
And then is just a memory from then and now

Sandy Feldmus

2018

control

I've lost all control
Spiraling, spiraling out of control
Like a mouse on a wheel
Or caged animal
Pacing, pacing in my mind

Let me off this ferris wheel
Fixes are so obvious
The worries don't stop
The parents, children, money and life
All coming at once

I was so good for so long
So strong, determined, full of strength and hope
Something clicked, changed in my brain
Like a tripped fuse switch
The power is out

The strength defused and gone
I've been so strong
No tears, no pain
Fight just fight

Don't invalidate my pain, my quiet, my suffering, my scars
How dare you judge my life and trauma?
Behold no bounty on my pain
Suppress your feelings
Oh no
Something opened the dam

Damn
It was all locked away
And now, now
The flood swells my brain
I cannot cry to let the dam open
Breathe, breathe, breathe

It will all work out, they say
Breathe

Silence

The silence is deafening
Trying to fill the void with small talk, but it's all
Me talking
No response
Oh wait
A reply
Good

Ow, it hurts, fuck, ow
Wait, did she say "fuck"?
She never cursed

I'm tired
Let's try
Okay
Seven minutes, I timed it
I videotaped it
Seven minutes to do a preschool puzzle

It goes here
No here
Oh, I did it
Yes, you did

Sandy Feldermus

Dead or Alive

Dead or alive? What is best?
Dead or alive? I do not jest
The sound of echoes in the halls
To sit and stare at the same four walls
Nothing is there, empty and hollow
Just watching and staring, a gaze to follow
A shadow that follows him around
Souls that forever will be bound

Stop talking and walking, chewing and sleeping
Your faculties are gone, we are all weeping
It cuts like a knife, so sharp and so painful
Dead or alive, the thoughts are shameful

What is best? To stay or to go?
What is best? We do not know
Does being here hold us together?
Does it make it all seem so much better?

This is not our choice or decision to make
But you must understand that our hearts do ache
You're not the one we once knew
The bond, the fabric, the ultimate glue

So, dead or alive? What is best?
Dead or alive? You decide the rest

Help

Sometimes I wonder what will be
Where I am, and what I'll see
What is the future? I need to know
What will life bring? My dreams, please show

Show me the way, my path, and my plight
What is my purpose, my goal, and my flight?

To create a life or a family?
Or to stop an unwinding calamity?
Of days gone by and a life no more
Why can't I see I can soar?

And be the friend, the mother, the spouse
And be the person without a rouse
Of a mind always spinning and moving around
Of thoughts coming and going, that have me so wound
Wound up in a ball
Chained to a fence
Of a life that looks perfect but makes no sense
No sense, why my thoughts are so sad and so strangling
No sense, why my thoughts are of a life that is dangling

Hold on, my friend, just a little more
The day will come, you will be free, and you'll soar
The noise will stop, just block the voices
The voices will stop, just make the choices
Set yourself free, just look ahead
You have a whole life to live, hold on by a thread

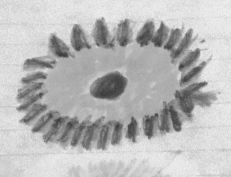

Sandy Feldmus

Just Because

Just because I appear so strong doesn't mean I am
Just because I appear so strong doesn't mean I can

You want my guidance and want to talk
To ask me questions and want to walk

But I'm hurting inside just as well
And my heart's beginning to swell

But I cannot let you see
What will become of me?

If you see what's going on in my heart, my soul, my mind
Perhaps you won't be so kind

To me, every day is a challenge, you should only know
The thoughts that rage inside my mind just won't let me go

Babe

The feeling of forgottenness
No one cares
Everyone is busy
Getting ready for another day
What about her?
She sits and cries
Yet nobody comes
Finally, someone she seems to know
She feels secure
Once again

She Died

Death, be not proud
Yet death must be proud

For it takes the lives of so many
Those afflicted with appalling disease or a hapless accident
Death has taken a life, a physical being, a soul
Yet one might die without the good fortune of a ripe old age
Where one may see the world, explore themselves
To see why they were put on this earth

Death is inevitable
We all must die
Death condemns our future too
Yet when those we love are physically gone
Do we have the right to feel sorry for them or for ourselves?
No one knows, for on the other side,
Can it not be a life more pleasing and free?

Turmoil

To most, my thoughts are not worth a single cent
My mind still wanders all about
These distant words are so distracting
The ones I loved, and who I thought loved me
I wish were concerned, yet my mind,
So entangled with perplexed thoughts, will not let me live
The conscience possesses my state of being
I want to be free with thoughts coming and going
With no recall of existence
So please stop this harassment

Sandy 2019

Cheryl 2019

Sandy
2019

I'm Stuck

Paralyzed with fear
My legs can't move, I'm stuck in cement
I try, but my mind controls my body,
Which controls my movements and actions
Why am I so fearful?
What's really going to happen?
I have my health, my family, my home, my life
Yet, there is a pervasive uneasiness
Why do others get to control our lives our livelihoods?
Why?
Why?
Why are people so mean, so nasty, so controlling
Their actions, their words, have so, so much power
Is karma real?
Will the world be right again?
Do people get their just dues?

My legs, they are so heavy
Stuck in a mud of emotions
And yet, my gut knows what's right
But it doesn't feel right
It doesn't feel
My life is about to explode
The world has gone mad

Please help me get off this merry go round of fear and disgust

Sandy

Secrets

Sweep it under the rug and it will go away
Sweep it under the rug the secrets of yesterday
If we don't speak of them, no one will know
The secrets we keep, the baggage in tow

Is it the childhood trauma or just a life of lies?
The secrets we keep can hurt and aren't wise
You perpetuate pain, tears, and hurt
Just deal with the issues, and be alert

To the problems you cause, the heartache you inflict
Hiding the lies is your way to trick
To trick yourself into thinking you're right
By hurting others in your self-preservation plight

Maybe it's your way to keep your world together
But the rug buckles over, no room for a feather
The people you hurt, the ones you want to save
Are those that will expose your secretive wave

A lifetime of lies and secrets are told
Isn't it time to just be bold?
And be your true self and know who you are
That you are imperfect and have a huge scar

Of your journey during the hardest of days
But the secrets you keep hurt in so many ways
Your children, your life, want to know
Why you need to carry this heavy tow

Of bondage to make your heart so heavy
Let it go now, unleash the levy
Of stories and lies, burdens and lore
The secrets you keep, the lies in store

[For Us]

What Can I Say?

What can I say?
What can I do?
I sit with the stillness of my thoughts
Racing through my mind
No rhyme or reason
No stopping them

Someone please help
Make them stop

I run
I run faster and faster
But they are still with me
The worries
They are still with me

Make them stop

Sandy Feldmus.

Embrace the Moment

Tragedy strikes when you least expect it
And then
You muster up the courage to fight through the pain
The hurt
And then, you cover the wounds so no one can see
You feel
The pain, the failure, the hurt
You cannot look at the wound
It so deeply penetrates your heart, your soul, your limbs
Only you know how to free it, to release the wound, the scar
So ugly, so grotesque, but so freeing
Survival, movement, motion, purpose
Purpose
You find a way to uncover the scar and look at it, embrace it for what it is
A lesson in patience, frustration, and loss of control
Embrace the moment

[For Me]

Embrace the moment
A lesson in patience, frustration, and loss of control
You find a way to uncover the scar and look at it, embrace it for what it is
Purpose
Survival, movement, motion, purpose
So ugly, so grotesque but so freeing
The scar

Only you know how to free it, to release the wound, the scar
It so deeply penetrates your heart, your soul, your limbs
You cannot look at the wound
You feel the pain, the failure, the hurt
You feel
And then, you cover the wounds so no one can see
The hurt

And then, you muster up the courage to fight the pain
And then,
Tragedy strikes when you least expect it

Embrace
the Moment
in Reverse

Memories

The precious memories of the days gone by
Recall the youth, the innocent youth
That must be lost but not forgotten
Remind us of the growth that must be nurtured yet never ending
Enhance our dreams that must yearn to come true
Arouse our desires that must not die
Restore our hopes that must be true
Renew a life that must be lived
And encourages a future that recalls the past
Yet stores those memories for the sake of tomorrow's existence

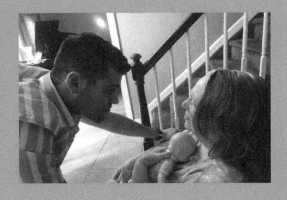
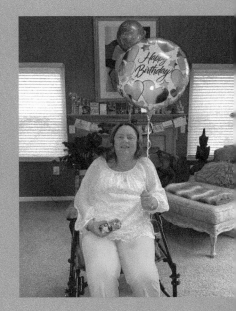

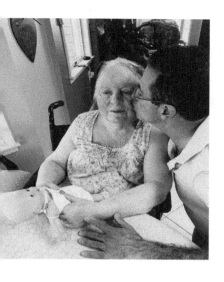

February 3rd, 1981

For all the times I've talked to you
For all the days I've prayed to you
For all the times I've respected you
I ask for one last chance

A chance to view the world
To review myself and my past
My family, my children, my friends
My car, my house, my life

My life

Doesn't it mean anything, anymore?
All I ask for is one last chance
To see the ocean, the mountains, the stars
To travel to all parts of the land
To watch the sunrise, the clouds disperse, and the final sunset
All I ask for is one last chance

[For Bubby Dora]

Thoughts

To describe how much I love you
It's hard for me to say
To tell you how much I'll miss you
My tears just run away
But the thoughts of the past will always remain
The good times and the bad
Remember the poem I wrote to you
Please try to be glad

I meant it forever more
But the memories will remain
The more I think the more I cry
So I'll end it on this refrain

Strength

Beauty is from within your eyes, your heart, and your soul.
It pains me to see you so sad, and in time, it will take its toll.
I'm here for you. I am your mom.
I'm here for you, to make you calm.

You are good and worthy through and through.
You're kind, considerate, and we all knew,
The person you are, the soul you've become,
To us, you're always number one.

But you need to learn to be true to yourself,
To trust your gut and take care of your health.
Life isn't easy, and it's not your fault,
When secrets are hidden in someone else's vault.

You are so loved and should not fear.
Life is hard and we are all here.
For your strength knows no bounds of eternal strife,
We just want you to trust yourself and enjoy your life.

[For Them]

My Loves

Would it matter if I'm here or not?
Would it matter if they forgot?
Who I am and what I want to be
I'm so lost without them, that's all I see
They are all that I wanted in my life
They bring so much joy despite the strife

I'm so happy for them as they move on
But they don't know that my role is gone
My heart is aching, my limbs are numb
Why do I feel this way? They are the sum

Of my entire existence, now what do I do?
I don't see a future, a hope, or a clue
What to do next? I knew this was coming
What to do next? What am I becoming?

Afraid to be alone, old and sad
Afraid to be alone, I don't know what will make me glad
Glad, happy or whole? What will it be?
So far in the future, I cannot see
Where I'm going. What is my plan?
All I wanted to do was to be their fan
So now, what do I do as they soar?
So proud, yet so sad, until I find my next door

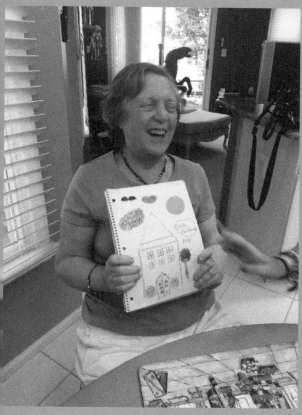

A Note from the Author

In March of 2020, just before the Covid pandemic, my dad told me he was taking my mom off her Alzheimer's medications. She was becoming verbally and physically abusive. She was later placed on hospice palliative care.

In July of 2020, she was diagnosed with pneumonia. With the fortitude and strength of my mother's wonderful aide Patricia, my sister and I escorted my mom from Florida to New Jersey. Masked and gloved up, we made the journey home.

But being home meant more than just being home. Alzheimer's just doesn't go away, but the decline can be kept at bay. Between visits 3-4 times a week, singing, dancing, doll therapy, talking into her face, refocusing her attention, feeding her, Sunday night family dinners, they all play a part in surrounding her with the love and warmth of her family. We found it kept the disease from rapidly progressing.

It's not just about being there and showing up. It's the constant interaction, whether she knows or not, can participate or not, or engage or not, that we believe found its way through the maze of the tangles and plaques of her brain. Perhaps, it touched the shoestrings of her heart. So, while we all think they are not in there, that they are content to sit all day and do nothing, with a little love in your voice, funny facial expressions, and a cheerful disposition, along with devotion and attention, you can find a moment that can create a memory for a life that still lives.

About the Author

Cheryl B. Kempner is a wife, mother of three, and retired attorney from Marlboro, New Jersey, whose vocations have always involved helping others. After leaving her career in law to focus on raising her three children, she found new ways to devote time to her passions.

For the past 15 years, Cheryl has been teaching Judaic and Hebrew studies to early learners and recently began an endeavor as an assistant Kindergarten teacher. She is also trained as a Literacy Volunteer and teaches ESL to adults through Literacy of New Jersey. Cheryl spends much of her time volunteering in various nursing homes, hospitals, and local organizations. She served as chairperson of the Marlboro Jewish Center Hospital Visitation Committee, board member of MJC Sisterhood, and the Social Action Committee.

Cheryl's affinity for writing has been innate to her since childhood. After her mother's diagnosis of dementia, Cheryl needed a place to put her feelings while adjusting to her mother's illness. While she'd been published for her writing of "Terror in the Skies: Who Should Pay the Price" in the *Syracuse Law School Journal of International Law and Commerce*, her creativity established a new purpose once Alzheimer's entered her family's world. Her recent work has been published with Alzheimer's Speaks.

Now, she's combining her poetry with her mother's artwork to bring forth a collection that raises awareness and pulls at your heartstrings. In her debut book, *Remember Me*, Cheryl takes her artistry--and her mother's--to new heights.

CPSIA information can be obtained
at www.ICGtesting.com
Printed in the USA
LVHW072355280322
714678LV00008B/146